How Do Airplanes Fly?

A Book about Airplanes

By Melvin and Gilda Berger
Illustrated by Paul Babb

Ideals Children's Books • Nashville, Tennessee

The authors, artist, and publisher wish to thank the following for their invaluable advice and instruction for this book:

Jane Hyman, B.S., M.Ed. (Reading), M.Ed. (Special Needs), C.A.E.S. (Supervisory and Curriculum Development)

Rose Feinberg, B.S., M.Ed. (Elementary Education), Ed.D. (Reading and Language Arts)

R.L. 2.2 Spache

Text copyright © 1996 by Melvin and Gilda Berger
Illustrations copyright © 1996 by Hambleton-Hill Publishing, Inc.

Published by Ideals Children's Books
An imprint of Hambleton-Hill Publishing, Inc.
Nashville, Tennessee 37218

Printed and bound in Mexico

Library of Congress Cataloging-in-Publication Data
Berger, Melvin.
     How do airplanes fly? : a book about airplanes / by Melvin and Gilda Berger ; illustrated by Paul Babb.
          p.   cm.—(Discovery readers)
     Includes index.
     Summary: Covers the history of flight, from Leonardo da Vinci to modern jumbo jets.
          ISBN 1-57102-058-6 (lib. bdg.)—ISBN 1-57102-044-6 (paper)
          1. Airplanes—Juvenile literature. 2. Flight—History—Juvenile literature.
     [1. Airplanes. 2. Flight—History.] I. Berger, Gilda. II. Babb, Paul, ill. III. Title.
     IV. Series.
     TL547.B4177   1996
     629.133'34—dc20   95-38469
                                                                              CIP
                                                                              AC

How Do Airplanes Fly? is part of the *Discovery Readers*® series.
Discovery Readers is a registered trademark of Hambleton-Hill Publishing, Inc.

You come to the airport.
It's a busy place.
Planes are flying overhead.
People are hurrying to catch their
    flights.

3

You go inside the airport.
A worker checks your ticket.
"Flight 125," she says.
That is the name of your flight.

She also checks your bag.
She will make sure it is put on the
    right airplane.
"Gate 4," she says. "Have a good
    flight."

GATES 1-15

FLT 125

You walk to Gate 4.
You will wait here until it is time to
get on the airplane.

Outside you can see the plane.
Wow!
It's as long as a football field.
It's as tall as a three-story house.

Cabin

This airplane can carry hundreds of
   people.
The people ride in the cabin (KAB-in).
It is near the middle of the plane.

Cargo Hold

The airplane can also carry tons of
   cargo (KAR-go).
Cargo can be bags, boxes, or crates.
The cargo is loaded into the bottom of
   the plane.
This is called the cargo hold.

As you watch, the pilots (PI-lets) go
into the plane.
There are three pilots.
The pilot flies the plane.
The copilot helps out.
The flight engineer (en-juh-NEER)
watches the instruments.

The pilots go into the cockpit.
The cockpit is at the front of the plane.
The pilots fly the plane from here.
There are lots of instruments in the
cockpit.

When the plane is very high in the air,
the pilots cannot see the ground.
They use the instruments in the cockpit
to guide the plane.
They also listen to radio signals.
These signals tell the pilots which
way to go.

9

You also see lots of other planes at
the airport.
They come in many different shapes
and sizes.
Some are waiting for fuel and
passengers (PAS-en-jurs).
Some are taking off.
And some are landing.

You can't help wondering.
How do airplanes fly?

Long ago there were no airplanes.
But people dreamed of flying.
"Birds can fly," they said.
"Why can't we?"

At first some people tied bird feathers
to their arms.
They waved their arms up and down.
But they were not able to fly.

Then about 500 years ago, someone
got a new idea.
His name was Leonardo da Vinci.
Leonardo was an inventor.
He was also a painter and a scientist.

Leonardo imagined a flying machine.
It had wings like a bird.
And they flapped like a bird's wings.
But Leonardo never tried it out.

Others thought of different ways to fly.
Two men in France flew in a giant
   balloon.
The balloon was filled with hot air.

The hot air made the balloon rise.
But a balloon is not an airplane.
It cannot always fly where you want
   to go.
A balloon must go wherever the wind
   blows it.

About 200 years ago, someone had
   another idea.
Make a flying machine with long
   wings.
These wings would not flap.
They would only help the machine
   stay up in the air.

This flying machine is called a glider
   (GLI-dur).
A glider is really an airplane without
   an engine.
The early gliders could fly.
And they could carry humans on short
   flights.

But gliders could not fly very far.
They could not stay up in the air for
   very long.

Then along came Orville and Wilbur
    Wright.

They were brothers.

They ran a bicycle shop in Ohio.

The brothers read about gliders.

They started building gliders too.

In 1903, the Wright brothers did
  something special.
They added an engine to their glider.
And they attached two propellers
  (pruh-PEL-urs) to the engine.

Hooray!
The Wright brothers had built the first
  airplane.
They named their invention *The Flyer*.

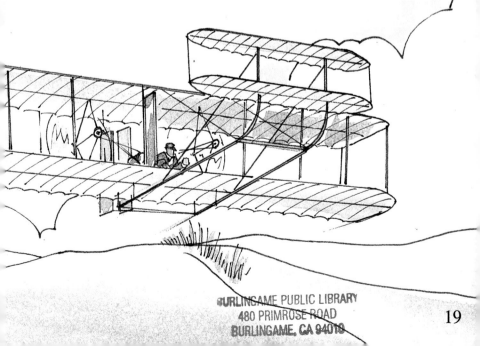

The Wright brothers tossed a coin.
The winner would fly the plane.
Orville won.

On December 17, 1903, Orville
    climbed into *The Flyer*.
The engine turned the propellers.
The propellers pulled the plane forward.
The plane moved faster and faster—
    and then it rose up into the air!

The first flight was at Kitty Hawk,
North Carolina.
It lasted only 12 seconds.
The plane flew only 120 feet.
The speed was only about 30 miles an
hour.
But now humans could fly in an
airplane!

Airplanes have changed a lot since
The Flyer.
Most of today's airplanes are
much bigger.

They are made of metal, not wood and
cloth like *The Flyer*.
They fly much, much faster.
And they fly much, much farther.

Each airplane is made of many, many
   parts.
The parts come from lots of small
   factories.
They arrive at a big factory.

Workers in the big factory fit the parts
together.
They test the plane.
Each part must work perfectly.

Modern propeller planes work the
same way as *The Flyer.*
An engine makes the propellers turn.
The propellers pull the airplane
forward.

The airplane rolls faster and faster.
Soon the wings lift it off the ground.
And the wings keep it in the air as it
flies away.

Modern propeller planes can go as fast
as 300 miles per hour.
And they can go as high as 6 1/2 miles
in the air.

Helicopters (HEL-uh-kop-turs) are like
  airplanes.
They work in much the same way as
  the propeller plane.
But there are some differences.

Helicopters
- —have no wings.
- —have a propeller on top, not in front.
- —can fly straight up and down.
- —can fly backward and sideways.
- —can hover, or stay in one place in the air.

Helicopters get their lift from a huge
propeller.
The propeller is on top.
It is called a rotor (RO-tur).
The rotor looks like a giant whirling
fan.

The pilot turns on the engine.
The engine makes the rotor spin.
This gives the helicopter its lift.
The rotor spins faster and faster.
The helicopter rises.

The pilot wants to move forward.
The rotor takes care of that job.
Tilt the rotor forward.
And the helicopter moves forward.

The pilot wants to move backward or
    to a side.
Tilt the rotor backward or to a side.
The helicopter flies backward or
    sideways.

Jet planes are also airplanes.
They are the newest kind of plane.
Jets can fly faster than propeller
　　planes.
Jets can reach speeds of over 600
　　miles an hour.

Jet planes can also fly higher.
They can fly 8 miles above the earth.

Jets have special engines.
They burn jet fuel.
The burning fuel forms a hot gas.
The hot gas takes up lots and lots of
space.

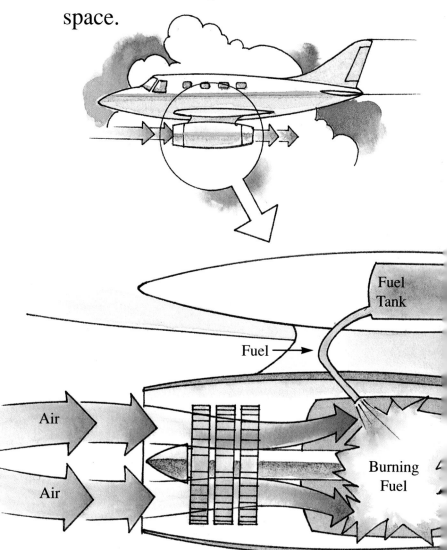

Fuel Tank

Fuel

Air

Air

Burning Fuel

The gas rushes out the back of the
    engine.
The gas moves very fast.
It pushes against the air.
This push sends the plane forward.

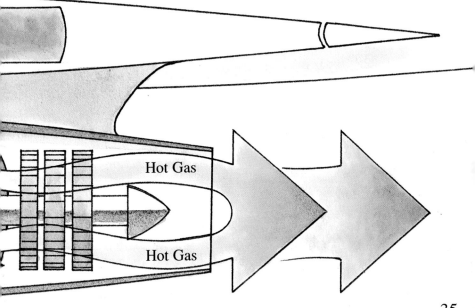

Hot Gas

Hot Gas

Use a small balloon to see how a jet
    engine works.
Blow up the balloon.
Hold the end closed with your fingers.

Now let go of the balloon.
What happens?
The balloon flies all around.

The balloon is really a tiny jet engine.
The air inside is like the hot gas in a
    jet engine.
The air is looking for a way to get out.
It rushes out of the end of the balloon
    at a high speed.
This sends the balloon flying.

air

Flight 125 is now ready.
It is time for you to climb into the
   airplane.
This airplane is a jet.

The cabin looks like the inside of a
   theater.
There are many rows of soft seats.
Larger planes will have more seats
   than smaller planes.

The flight attendant works on the
    plane.
She helps you find your seat.
You sit down and fasten your seat belt.
You wait for the plane to take off.

The plane starts to move.

You look out of the window.

Hot gases are rushing out of the jet engines.

They push the plane forward.

The plane moves slowly down the
    runway.
It picks up speed.
Faster and faster it goes.

Watch the back sides of the wings.
You will see some flaps that bend down.
They help the plane lift up off the
ground.

The plane slowly rises.
The wings hold it up in the air.
The jet engines push it forward.

43

Higher and higher the plane rises.
Look out of the window at the ground
below.
Big buildings look like postage
stamps.

You can see long roads stretching out.
You can see tiny cars on the roads.

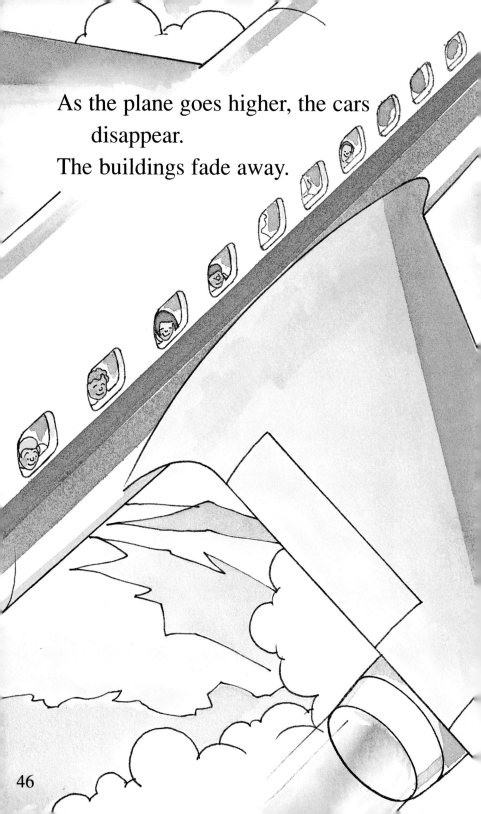

As the plane goes higher, the cars disappear.
The buildings fade away.

Soon you are up in the clouds.
You cannot see the land at all.
You are flying like a bird.
Happy landing!

Index